ITALY

SALLY GARRINGTON

Facts On File, Inc.

Italy

Copyright © 2004 by Evans Brothers Limited

All rights reserved. No part of this book may be reproduced or utilized in any form or by any means, electronic or mechanical, including photocopying, recording, or by any information storage or retrieval systems, without permission in writing from the publisher. For information contact:

Facts On File, Inc.
132 West 31st Street
New York NY 10001

Library of Congress Cataloging-in-Publication Data

Garrington, Sally.
  Italy / Sally Garrington.
    p. cm. — (Countries of the world)
  First published: London: Evans Brothers, 2004.
  Includes index.
  Contents: Introducing Italy—Landscape and climate—Italy's resources—Italy's economy—Infrastructure—The people of Italy—The environment—Challenges of the future.
  ISBN 0-8160-5502-5 (hc)
  1. Italy—Juvenile literature. I. Title. II. Countries of the world (Facts On File, Inc.)

DG417.G28 2004
945—dc22   2004047093

Facts On File books are available at special discounts when purchased in bulk quantities for businesses, associations, institutions, or sales promotions. Please call our Special Sales Department in New York at (212) 967-8800 or (800) 322-8755.

Endpapers (front): A view of the dramatic Colosseum, in Rome.
Title page: Traders at the flower market in Naples.
Imprint and Contents page: A row of gondolas in Venice at dusk.
Endpapers (back): The unique mast sculpture by artist Renzo Piano on Genoa's harborfront.

You can find Facts On File on the World Wide Web at http://www.factsonfile.com.

Printed in China by Imago

10 9 8 7 6 5 4 3 2 1

Editor:	Katie Orchard
Designer:	Jane Hawkins
Map artwork:	Peter Bull
Charts and graphs:	Encompass Graphics, Ltd.
Photographs:	all by Edward Parker except front endpapers, 6–7 (Corbis Digital Stock); 44 bottom (Peter Frischmuth).

First published by Evans Brothers Limited, 2A Portman Mansions, Chiltern Street, London W1U 6NR, United Kingdom.

This edition published under license from Evans Brothers Limited. All rights reserved.

The Italian flag is based on the French flag, the tricolore, but instead of a blue stripe, it has a green stripe. It was adopted as the national flag in 1946, when Italy became a republic.

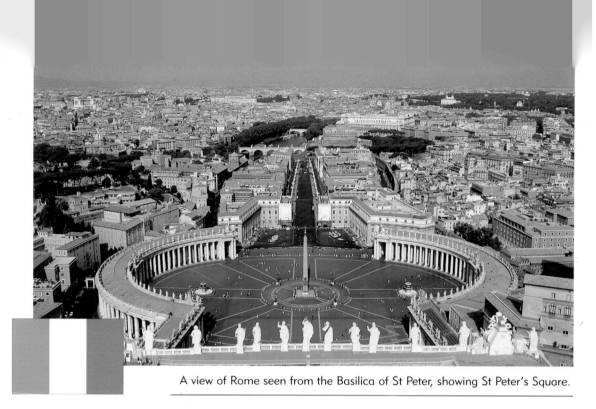

A view of Rome seen from the Basilica of St Peter, showing St Peter's Square.

Italy as we know it today is a young country – it was not unified until 1861. Within its 21 regions there is a rich diversity of culture, architecture and landscapes. Italy is also one of the most urbanized countries in Europe after the United Kingdom, Belgium and Germany.

Italy is located in southern Europe and has borders with Austria, Slovenia, Switzerland and France. Its northern regions are divided from the rest of the continent by the Alps. The boot-shaped peninsula juts out into the Mediterranean Sea. At its "toe" is the island of Sicily, with the island of Sardinia farther to the north and west.

Within the Republic of Italy there are two independent states: the Vatican, residence of the Pope and located within Rome; and the Republic of San Marino, Europe's smallest republic.

People sometimes say there are two Italies, one being the more industrialized and wealthy northern region centered around Milan. The other is the southern region, which is less developed and more dependent on agriculture and has a lower income per person, although this situation is changing.

A COLORFUL HISTORY

Although young as a united country, the land of Italy has a history stretching back more than 3,000 years. The Roman Empire had a widespread influence in Europe and beyond. The empire left behind a legacy of road and city building as well as engineering projects, including aqueducts. After the collapse of the empire in A.D. 476, many groups invaded, among them Germans and Muslim Arabs. In the twelfth century came the rise of the city-states, when cities such as Venice, Florence and Genoa became independent and very powerful. Later Italy was controlled by the Spanish, the Austrians and finally the French under the command of Napoleon. All of these influences have left their mark on the culture and architecture of the country.

In the nineteenth century, Giuseppe Garibaldi helped to create a unified and independent country. Since the Second World War, Italy has seen many changes of government, none of which has managed to prevent the sense that Italy is still a country of two halves. Despite this division, the country has the world's eighth-largest

St Mark's Square in Venice is a major attraction for visitors to the city – and pigeons!

economy. In 1957, Italy became a founding member of the European Community, which later became the European Union (EU).

THE PRESENT DAY

The Italians are a passionate and lively people with a great sense of style. The country itself has a rich cultural heritage and a broad range of natural landscapes. These factors continue to attract people to Italy as both a vacation destination and a home.

Italian people have a reputation for fashion and design. Many of the world's top fashion houses are Italian.

KEY DATA

Official Name:	The Republic of Italy
Area:	301,300km²
Population:	57,844,000
Main Cities:	Rome, Milan, Naples, Turin, Palermo, Genoa
GDP Per Capita (2001)*	US$24,510
Currency:	Euro (€)
Exchange Rate:	US$1 = €0.81
	£1 = €1.49

* Calculated on Purchasing Power Parity basis
Source: World Bank

Monte Bianco towers above the high Alps in the northwest of the country.

Italy is made up of a continental northern section and a relatively narrow peninsula section that juts out into the Mediterranean Sea. The peninsula divides the Mediterranean into the Tyrrhenian Sea to the west and the Adriatic Sea to the east. The country can be divided into five main landscape regions: the Alps, the Po-Venetia plain, the Apennines, the coastal plains and the islands.

THE ALPS

The Alps are fold mountains that connect the northern border of Italy with the rest of Europe. The highest point is Monte Bianco (Mont Blanc) at 4,807m, which rises on the French-Italian border. The eastern Alps are called the Dolomites.

Within the Alps there are many glaciers. The largest is the Miage Glacier on the slopes of Monte Bianco, which is 10km long. The sources of the Po, Ticino, Adige and Piave Rivers are all on the south-facing slopes of the Alps. On the lower slopes of the Alps are large lakes, formed by the retreat of glaciers thousands of years ago. The three largest lakes are Lake Maggiore, Lake Como and Lake Garda.

RELIEF MAP

GERMANY

LIECHTENSTEIN

AUSTRIA

SWITZERLAND

SLOVENIA

FRANCE

Monte Bianco (4,807m)

Lake Maggiore

Lake Como

Lake Garda

DOLOMITES

Val di Fiemne

Ticino

Adda

Adige

Venice

CROATIA

Turin

Po

Po-Venetia Plain

SAN MARINO

BOSNIA - HERZEGOVINA

LIGURIAN SEA

Arno

Florence

Livorno

Tiber

APPENNINES

ADRIATIC SEA

Elba

Corno Grande (2,912m)

CORSICA (FRANCE)

Rome

Ofanto

Naples

Pontine Islands

Capri

Mt Vesuvius (1,218m)

Val d'Agri

SARDINIA

TYRRHENIAN SEA

Cagliari

Stromboli

Aeolian Islands

Vulcano

MEDITERRANEAN SEA

Palermo

SICILY

Mt Etna (3,323m)

Strait of Messina

0   200km

0   100 miles

N

Vegetation in the Alpine region changes according to altitude, with trees on the lower slopes and alpine meadows and tundra high up in the mountains.

THE PO-VENETIA PLAIN

The Po-Venetia plain is the largest lowland area in Italy. It follows the line of the Po valley to the Adriatic coast, where the river has created a large delta over time. Other rivers, including the Adige and Tagliamento, have also helped build up the sediments of the delta. The large plain was once part of the Adriatic Sea. Today, the plain is densely populated. Little of the natural vegetation of willows, alders and oaks remains.

THE APENNINES

The Apennine mountain range is often called "the backbone of Italy." For much of the peninsula the Apennines run parallel to the coast, but they are cut by valleys such as the Valle del Volturno in the south. Many rivers run east and west from these mountains, but they are much shorter than those flowing from the Alps. The highest peak in this region is the Corno Grande, in Gran Sasso d'Italia, at 2,912m. Much of this mountainous area has been deforested and overgrazed by sheep and goats. Heavy winter rains wash away the soil and reduce the fertility of the area.

COASTAL PLAINS

To the west and east of the Apennines are Italy's coastal plains. These are more extensive on the western side and run from Naples up to Livorno. The plain of the Arno River extends from the coast inland towards Florence. This large river plain is heavily populated. The plains around Naples are ideal for farming as they provide flat, fertile land with a warm Mediterranean climate.

THE ISLANDS

Italy has many islands, the two largest and most important of which are Sicily and Sardinia. The Apennines reach into northern Sicily, and Mount Etna, a volcano, is located in the east of the island. The center of Sicily is a large plateau. Sardinia has a mountainous interior with coastal plains, which are widest on the west coast.

Italy has many other small islands, mainly in the Tyrrhenian Sea. These include the Aeolian Islands, Capri, the Pontine Islands and Elba. Most of these islands rely on tourism as their main source of income.

The black sands on this beach on Stromboli show the island's volcanic origins.

VOLCANOES AND EARTHQUAKES

Italy has a major plate margin running through it, marking the boundary between two sections of the Earth's crust that are moving in different directions. The Adriatic Plate is part of the African Plate, which is slowly moving northward, whereas the Eurasian Plate is moving southward. These movements often result in earthquakes. In the Alps earthquakes are sometimes felt as the two plates continue to collide and land is forced upward. The Alps are still growing in height from this movement. In some areas, where one plate is forced beneath the Earth's surface as it meets another plate, magma can sometimes find its way to the surface and create volcanoes.

Volcanoes and earthquakes have affected Italy throughout its history, from the famous eruption of Vesuvius and the destruction of Pompeii in A.D. 79 to the major Assisi earthquake in 1997. The most recent dramatic volcanic eruption was Mount Etna's outpouring in 2002.

CASE STUDY
SAN GIULIANO EARTHQUAKE

On 31 October 2002 an earthquake of 5.4 on the Richter scale struck the village of San Giuliano in the Molise region. It caused 29 deaths, most of which occurred within the Francesco Iovine School. The school had been built in the 1950s, before there were strict building regulations for areas that were likely to suffer earthquakes. During this period, poor design and shoddy materials were used. The concrete roof was too heavy, and within seconds the poorly constructed walls gave way and the roof crashed down, killing 26 students and their teacher. Other, much older buildings in the village suffered little or no damage.

The volcano on Stromboli island erupts several times an hour. It has been erupting this frequently for the last 160,000 years!

VOLCANOES, PLATES AND MOUNTAINS

The ruins of Pompeii attract tourists who want to see the remains of this once-thriving Roman town.

CASE STUDY
MOUNT ETNA

Ash and steam rise from Mount Etna – a constant threat to people living on its slopes.

Mount Etna, on the island of Sicily, is Europe's largest land-based volcano. It is located where the African and Eurasian plates meet. Etna erupts frequently. One million people live on the flanks of the volcano, attracted by the very fertile soils found there. They have learned to live with the constant threat of eruption from Etna. There was a major eruption period between 1992 and 1993, and in 2002 another period of volcanic activity occurred.

The volcano had shown signs of activity during the summer of 2002, and then on 27 October it erupted. This eruption was accompanied by many earthquakes, which continued for several days, reaching up to 4.3 on the Richter scale. During the eruption, two streams of lava flowed down the north and south slopes of the volcano. Molten rock was propelled up to 300 meters into the air, and large areas of pine forest were set on fire by the hot lava. Heavy ash falls covered nearby villages and the town of Catania, and about 100 homes were damaged by earthquakes. In an effort to minimize the potential damage, local authorities evacuated 1,000 people from their homes. Workers dug channels to divert lava from villages, and water-carrying planes stood by, ready to put out fires.

RIVERS

Rivers that originate in the Alps, such as the Ticino and Po, have large basins and flow across the Po plain to the sea. These rivers flow all year round, fed by rains in autumn and spring and by melting glaciers in summer.

In the peninsula section of Italy, rivers flow east and west from the Apennine watershed (boundary between drainage basins). The peninsula is narrow, so these rivers are much shorter than those in the north. The flow of rivers such as the Ofanto in southern Italy depends entirely on rainfall, which can be heavy during spring and autumn, causing flash flooding. However, in the summer, rainfall can be so low that the rivers dry up completely.

PROBLEMS OF LOW FLOW

Italy's climate is characterized by summer drought, especially in the south. This problem has become worse over the last decade, partly due to global warming and partly because there has been a 25 percent decline in annual average rainfall.

The water supply system, particularly in the south, is very inefficient. Approximately 60 percent of Italians suffer some form of water shortage for

LEFT: A waterfall in the Alps flows into a pool on its way down to the plains.

BELOW: Low flow in a river in Tuscany.

three months of the year. To combat this problem, aqueducts have been built to transfer water from the wetter areas in the mountains to the drier regions of the south such as Basilicata and Puglia, which receive only 550mm of rain each year. The Puglia Aqueduct transfers water from springs in the Apennines to Puglia via 247km of pipeline and through numerous tunnels.

FLOODING

With an increase in extreme weather conditions linked to global warming, Italy has suffered several disastrous floods over the last decade, including those in the Piemonte region in 1994 when 94 people were killed. In 2000 the Ticino and Po Rivers flooded in the north of Italy and 20 people were killed. At the same time 15 campers were killed in a flash flood in the south of the country. Part of the problem is that there has been an increase in building on the floodplain. This means that the land surface is paved over and can no longer absorb water. There has also been large-scale deforestation on mountain slopes. This results in less rainfall being intercepted and absorbed by trees. Instead it speeds over the surface to the rivers and floods occur. Coupled with this the surface water picks up soil particles and transports them to the river, where they add to the riverbed, raising it and making the river more likely to flood.

This dried up river near Malazzo, Sicily, shows the impact of a summer drought.

2002 DROUGHT

In 2002 Italy suffered the worst drought in 50 years.

IMPACTS OF DROUGHT

- Farmers lost €3.5 billion (about US$4.4 billion), with thousands of hectares of crops destroyed.
- Hospitals ran out of water and had to get the fire brigade to transport some.
- Lake levels declined, even in the north of the country.
- Areas of desertification increased in the south
- Water was being stolen and resold.
- People in towns often had water on tap for a only couple of hours a day.

SOLUTIONS

- Make urgent repairs to existing water supply systems to reduce losses through leakage.
- Launch an education campaign to promote more sustainable use of water.
- Change crop types to ones that require less water.
- Introduce legislation to encourage industries to recycle water.
- Set up planned measures for rationing during future droughts.
- Replant watersheds to encourage retention of water within the landscape.
- Reintroduce terracing to help absorb rainfall naturally.

The Dora Baltea forms a tributary of the Po River as it flows from the Alps.

The Po River is the longest river in Italy. It flows for 650km from its source in the western Alps to its delta on the Adriatic Sea in the east of the country. Its main tributaries also have their source in the Alps and include the Ticino, Adda and Dora Baltea Rivers. The Po's drainage basin covers 70,000km² and forms 24 percent of Italy's land surface. The area has a population of 16 million inhabitants, and 44 percent of it is used for farming. More than half of the crops are irrigated using water from the Po and its tributaries. Water is also extracted from the river for domestic and industrial use.

UPPER COURSE

The upper reaches of the Po have steep slopes, where the river flows at high speed and there is much erosion. In the first 35km of its channel, the Po River falls 1,700 meters with many rapids and waterfalls. This energy is harnessed by many hydroelectric power (HEP) stations: Within its basin there are 269! The Adda River alone has eight HEP stations in its upper reaches. But the dams linked to the power stations have caused changes to the river ecosystems by altering the water flow. Another problem is that the material eroded from the Alps by the fast-flowing river is dropped as the river enters the reservoirs behind the dams and loses energy. These reservoirs are gradually filling up with sediment and cannot store as much water.

MIDDLE SECTION

From Turin, the Po crosses its huge plain. It is here that human impact is greatest. The river used to meander across the floodplain but now for much of its course it has been straightened and is held in by levees (embankments) to prevent the river from flooding and changing its course. This means that in times of high water flow the river

cannot absorb the excess on its floodplain, which is now used for industry, housing and intensive agriculture. Irrigated rice farming is important here, and chemical fertilizer is applied regularly. Consequently, there is a runoff of nitrates into the river, causing pollution. There are many chemical pollutants from the industries that line the river in Milan and Turin. Another source of pollution is domestic sewage. Through 2004, Milan still pumped most of the city's untreated human waste into the river, which carries it down to the delta.

THE DELTA

The Po delta is where much of the material eroded from the Alps and Apennines is deposited. Farmland has been reclaimed from its marshes over the last 300 years and it is a productive rice-growing area. Fish farming of sea bass and shellfish is also an important industry (although this has been affected by pollution from the cities of the plain).

When the Po River reaches Turin, it flows past many industrial buildings. Pollution can be a major problem here.

However, the delta is also an important area for wildlife, particularly breeding and migrating birds. Environmentalists are working to allow some reclaimed land to flood once again to provide an increasingly rare wetland habitat. They see conservation tourism as a way of providing new jobs within the proposed Po Delta National Park. Not surprisingly, this plan is not popular with farmers!

There is now a government-funded Po Basin Plan which is carrying out research and monitoring of the Po River. Eventually, this will lead to tougher pollution legislation and more sustainable ways of managing the river's channel.

Tourists wait for a boat to take them on to the Po delta, where they will see rare wetland ecosystems.

CLIMATE

Italy has a wide range of climates, from the cool alpine region in the north to the warm Mediterranean peninsula region with its summer droughts. Regional winds can affect the climates of some areas. The Sirocco Wind is a hot, dry wind that blows from the deserts of North Africa in the summer and can add to the problems of Italy's summer drought. In spring, areas in southern peninsular Italy and Sardinia can be affected by the Mistral Wind, a cold, dry wind that blows off the continent of Europe and is sometimes responsible for extensive crop damage.

MOUNTAIN CLIMATES

In the Alps and in the Apennines the climate changes with altitude. Broad-leaved deciduous trees such as oaks grow in the valleys, where the climate is less harsh with warmer temperatures. Farther up the mountains are pine trees, which can cope with the colder and windier conditions found there. Above 2,000m (the tree line), it is too windy and cold for any trees to grow, but there are alpine

The upper reaches of the Val D'Aosta are bare, while meadow plants thrive lower down.

meadows made up of grasses and flowering plants. Above these, but below the snowline, is a zone of alpine tundra with waterlogged soils in which mosses, lichens and tussock grasses grow.

In the summer, heat can build up above the south-facing slopes of the Alps and there are many thunderstorms, which give this area its peak rainfall.

CASE STUDY
SEVERE STORMS IN NORTHERN ITALY

On 4 August 2002, there was a particularly severe thunder and hail storm on the northern Po plain. There had been a heat wave, and the strong upward movement of air caused violent thunderstorms with gales, heavy rain and hail. Hailstones weighing up to 700g were recorded – nearly as heavy as five baseballs! About 20 percent of the fruit and olive harvest was destroyed, and vineyards near Lake Garda were severely damaged. Trees were blown down across roads and railways, and electricity supplies were disrupted. Hundreds of cars were damaged and 30 people were injured by hailstones.

THE NORTHERN PLAIN

The large northern plain is surrounded on three sides by mountains and the Apennine range prevents the warm sea breezes reaching the area. Autumn and winter are also characterized by fogs forming over the moist land. There are few strong winds here because the area is sheltered by the surrounding mountains, so the fog does not readily disperse. In the summer months heat builds up, leading to strong upward movements of air, causing many thunderstorms. The natural vegetation of this relatively flat plain includes moisture-loving willows and alders.

COASTAL AREAS

The coastal areas of Italy have a smaller temperature range than the interior regions. The Mediterranean Sea heats up slowly during the summer and releases this heat during the winter. It has the effect of keeping the temperatures of the coastal areas more even.

The eastern coasts are cooler than those of the west because the prevailing winds come from the northeast and tend to be

Long, hot summers and sandy beaches attract large numbers of vacationers to the Mediterranean coasts.

colder. The Mediterranean Sea on the eastern side of Italy (the Adriatic) is shallower and thus does not store heat so well. The winds from over this part of the Mediterranean Sea do not even out the temperatures as well as those in the west.

TEMPERATURE AND RAINFALL

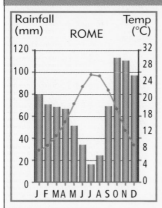

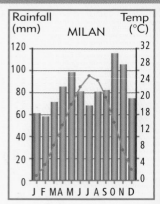

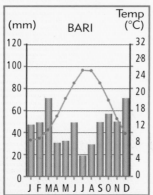

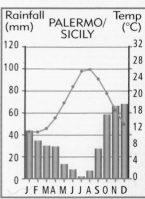

KEY:
Temperature
Rainfall

Marble has been extracted from quarries around Carrara for more than 2,000 years.

Italy is quite a young region in term of its geology, and because of this the country does not have large deposits of minerals and ores. In the past, this lack slowed Italy's development. The country has declining reserves of oil and gas, and its coal deposits are minor compared with other sources. However, Italy does have thriving timber and fishing industries.

RAW MATERIALS

Volcanic activity has left large deposits of sulfur, such as at Barrafranca on the island of Sicily. Sulfur is used mainly in the manufacture of sulfuric acid. This is an important material in the paint industry and in the manufacture of explosives. Bauxite ore, from which aluminum is made, is mined on the Gargano Peninsula in eastern Italy. Apart from feldspar, which is used in the glass and ceramic industry, the mineral deposits are very small and Italian industry relies heavily on imports.

Over time heat and pressure deep underground have changed limestone deposits into marble. The finest white marble in the world is found at Carrara, in Tuscany, where it has been quarried since Roman times. It was used by Michelangelo for his statue of David and is still the marble of choice for many modern sculptors.

FORESTRY

Italy has 10 percent of the world's cork oak forests. Around 20,000 tonnes of cork are produced each year, and Italy is the third most important producer after Portugal and Spain. Cork oaks are found especially in the Lombardia region. A cork oak begins producing cork when it is 20 years old and usually lives for 150 years. The cork comes from the outer bark, which is stripped away with great care and taken away to be processed. Over the next five years, the tree will grow a new outer layer, which can then be harvested again.

Around 33 percent of Italy is forested. (US forest cover is about 22 percent.) Timber is an important resource for Italy. It is harvested mainly in the northern half of the country. The timber sector contributes 10 percent to the national economy.

This timber yard in Piemonte processes trees that have been harvested in the region.

FEATURES OF A MULTIPURPOSE FOREST

- Some areas are used for commercial timber production.
- Access is allowed to the public for recreation activities such as fishing, hiking, and mushroom harvesting.
- Some areas are designated as habitat reserves, where minimal management takes place. The aim of this is to support local wildlife.
- In a larger forest, there may also be a visitor center.

Some older forests are owned and run by the community, such as in the Val di Fiemme, in the southeastern Alps. Trees are harvested in small areas, which are clear-cut, prepared and then replanted. There is a move within these community forests toward multiple use of the forest area (see box on this page). This has already been happening in the publicly owned forests, but the aim in the community forests has been mainly timber production.

FISHING

Fishing is an important industry in Italy, especially around the islands of Sicily and Sardinia. Here sardines and bluefin tuna are caught and processed. However, there is growing concern about the level of the fish stocks in the Mediterranean Sea, and catches have been declining. The EU is proposing drastic cuts to the amount fishermen are allowed to catch in order to maintain fish stocks in the future.

Tuna and octopus for sale in a fish market, in Palermo, Sicily.

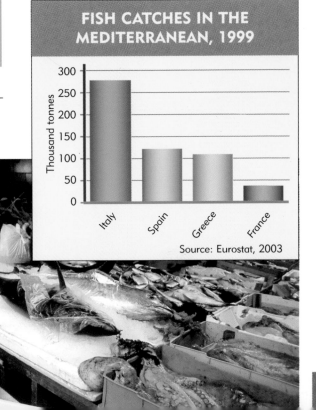

FISH CATCHES IN THE MEDITERRANEAN, 1999

Thousand tonnes

Italy, Spain, Greece, France

Source: Eurostat, 2003

ENERGY

Italy has a high rate of energy consumption linked to its strong economy. However, the country has little in the way of fossil fuel reserves and is very dependent on imports for its energy supplies. Italy is trying to rely less heavily on imports of fossil fuels, partially because several of the countries upon which it depends are in the less politically stable areas of the world such as North Africa and the Middle East. Italy has also signed the Kyoto Protocol, which means that it is committed to reducing carbon emissions (linked to fossil fuel use) over the next decade.

COAL, OIL AND GAS

Italy has very little coal of its own and has to import it from South Africa, Indonesia and Australia. Coal makes up only 6 percent of the energy demand and is used mainly in electricity generation. Italy is one of the largest oil consumers in Western Europe, and 95 percent of the oil consumed is imported, largely from North Africa and the Middle East. Natural gas is also imported from countries such as Russia and Norway by pipeline. There is also a pipeline from North Africa under the Mediterranean Sea to Sicily.

Italy does have some oil and gas reserves of its own. Oil is found on the island of Sicily and offshore. New onshore reserves are being developed at Val d'Agri, in the southern Apennines, and a pipeline has been built to connect it to the Taranto refinery. Gas fields are found mainly in the Po valley, and others are located in the Adriatic Sea.

NUCLEAR POWER

Although Italy has four nuclear power plants, none of them is producing electricity. After the disaster at Chernobyl in the former USSR in 1986, Italians voted in 1987 to abandon nuclear power. The power stations have been maintained because they contain harmful wastes, which must be monitored. The Italian government recently moved to allow the power plants to be used once again to produce electricity. This is because they produce no carbon emissions and would help in keeping to the Kyoto Protocol.

RENEWABLE ENERGY

Hydroelectric power (HEP) is the most important of Italy's renewable energy resources. Although they are expensive to build and have a considerable impact on mountain ecosystems, once they are up and running HEP stations provide a sustainable form of power.

This oil refinery at Taranto processes mostly imported oil.

POWER FROM BENEATH THE EARTH'S SURFACE

Italy led the world in geothermal power production when the first geothermal power plant was commissioned in 1904 in Larderello. It remained the only one in the world until 1958! The Larderello plant pumps steam from deep, heated underground sources, where water is under high pressure. When this superheated steam reaches the surface, it drives turbines to create electricity.

Wind generators in Abruzzo provide a nonpolluting alternative energy source to fossil fuels.

The Italian government is investing heavily in research into solar and wind power. The Vasto Plant in Abruzzo is the first large-scale solar power plant in Europe. The government has also recently launched its "10,000 Rooftops" program, which aims to subsidize the construction of banks of photovoltaic (solar) cells on the roofs of people's houses in order to reduce fossil fuel demand.

Wind power is being harnessed in the Apennine region and now there are plans to construct wind farms offshore in the southwest.

This HEP station in the Val d'Aosta in the Alps provides a clean, renewable energy supply for buildings in the surrounding area.

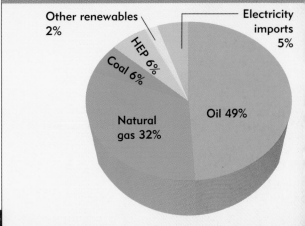

ENERGY CONSUMPTION, 2001 (% OF TOTAL)

- Other renewables 2%
- HEP 6%
- Coal 6%
- Natural gas 32%
- Oil 49%
- Electricity imports 5%

Beans and corn grow on a farm in Piemonte. Agricultural output is high in this area.

AGRICULTURE

Agricultural activities in Italy depend on the climate and landscape of the various regions, but other factors are also important, such as closeness to transport networks and markets, and the influence of European Union legislation. About 5 percent of Italy's population work in the agricultural sector, but it contributes only 2 percent of the nation's gross domestic product, or GDP.

MOUNTAINOUS FARMING

Farms tend to be smaller in upland areas and they are more likely to be family run. Steep slopes, a harsher climate and poor soils mean that mountainous areas are largely used for raising livestock rather than

AGRICULTURAL LAND USE

Irrigated area
Major rice growing area
Vines and olives
Livestock
Cereal and dairy farming
Citrus groves (oranges and lemons)

SWITZERLAND
AUSTRIA
SLOVENIA
FRANCE
Turin
CROATIA
San Remo
SAN MARINO
Ventimiglia
ADRIATIC SEA
LIGURIAN SEA
N
CORSICA (FRANCE)
Naples
SARDINIA
TYRRHENIAN SEA
MEDITERRANEAN SEA
SICILY

0   200km
0   100 miles

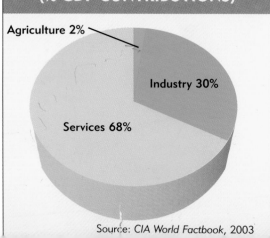

ECONOMIC STRUCTURE, 2001 (% GDP CONTRIBUTIONS)

Agriculture 2%
Industry 30%
Services 68%

Source: *CIA World Factbook, 2003*

growing crops. In the Alpine region drought is not normally a problem, so lush grass can grow on the slopes. Cattle are raised here. In the drier Apennines sheep farming is more common because sheep can thrive on poorer pasture. Vines are grown on south-facing slopes, and fodder crops are grown for the animals in the Alps and Apennines.

THE IRRIGATED PLAINS

The most productive agricultural region is in the more industrial north, on the plain of the Po. The area receives rain all year and has fertile soils. Its productivity is enhanced by further irrigation, which leads to high yields of wheat and rice. Farms in this region are generally larger than those in the rest of Italy and there are more agribusinesses (large-scale commercial farms). Coastal plains near Naples also use irrigation and this, coupled with the fertile volcanic soils of the region, means that vegetables, fruit and cereals can be grown. Irrigation in northeastern Sicily enables commercial production of lemons to take place.

CASE STUDY
FLOWER PRODUCTION AROUND SAN REMO

The area from Genoa to Ventimiglia on the Italian-French border is known as the *Riviera dei Fiori*, or the Coast of Flowers, with its center at San Remo. The mild climate encourages the production of cut flowers, such as carnations and roses, and potted plants, including geraniums. Growers have adapted the hilly landscape by cutting terraces to create small areas of flat land on which the flowers are grown. Most of the flower producers are very small firms, which join together to form cooperatives to market their produce. San Remo's flower market is the most important in southern Europe and has good links to the rest of the continent.

COASTAL AGRICULTURE

Around the coasts of Italy the traditional Mediterranean olive trees and vines are found. Farther south, citrus groves also thrive, and in the northwest, flower production is important. Crops benefit from the very mild winters and warm, dry summers, although drought can be a problem.

CASE STUDY
WINE PRODUCTION

Italy has the second-largest crop of grapes in the world and produces more than 20 percent of the world's output of wine. The vines need brief but cold winters to kill off pests and warm summers to ripen the grapes. They grow best on south- or southeast-facing slopes and need to have well-drained soils. Much of Italy is used for growing vines, although most producers are small scale. There are more than 50,000 individual wine producers in Italy. Most family farms have a few vines on a small terrace of land just to provide wine for the family table. Red and white wines are produced. Italy's most famous wine is probably Chianti, a red wine produced in Tuscany, but there are hundreds of others. Two popular wines, Soave and Valpolicella, are also produced on an industrial scale and are widely exported.

Terraced vineyards in Barolo, Piemonte – an important region for wine production.

Leather jackets for sale on a market stall. Italy has many factories producing leather goods.

MANUFACTURING

Northern Italy is part of Europe's core area and is home to more than half of Italy's manufacturing output. Its residents enjoy a higher income and lower unemployment rates than the south. The southern regions are known collectively as the *Mezzogiorno*, or "land of the midday sun." They are located on the peninsula of Italy and make up part of Europe's periphery, an outer region suffering from high unemployment. Although manufacturing and services are the largest sectors of the economy in this area, agriculture remains more important in terms of employment here than in the north.

THE NORTHERN POWERHOUSE

Northern Italy developed earlier than the south because of its trading links across the Alps and its fertile agricultural land in the Po basin. Milan grew because of this trade and is now the country's most important financial and business center, home to the Italian Stock Exchange – the *Borsa*. Alpine streams provided early waterpower for the development of the textile industry. This eventually led to the development of the fashion industry based in Milan, which rivals Paris in its importance. Today Milan not only produces designer fashion but excels at manufacturing high-quality, mass-produced clothing. Famous Italian design houses include Valentino, Versace and Armani.

Wealth brought by the textile industry allowed the region to diversify its industries, and engineering design and manufacture became important in the twentieth century. Car manufacturing grew up around the city of Turin. Component manufacturers moved into the region to supply firms such as Fiat. Engineering continues to grow in this region because of a skilled workforce, good transport routes and the presence of similar companies.

CASE STUDY
FURNITURE CLUSTER AROUND TREVISO

Italy is famous for good quality, well-designed furniture. The industry is made up of many small firms, which specialize in different stages of product development. In Treviso, kitchen and office furniture is made, with one company specializing in the production of the doors, another the work surfaces and yet another the handles. There are 606 small firms in Treviso concerned with the manufacture of furniture!

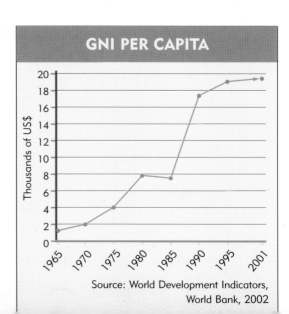

GNI PER CAPITA

Source: World Development Indicators, World Bank, 2002

This chemical factory in Bergamo has been built close to important high-speed road networks.

Although high-tech industries have suffered recently worldwide, they are an important sector within Italy's industries. Italy has the fourth-highest employment rate in high-tech industries within the EU. More than 21,000 people were employed in this sector in 2000. These firms tend to cluster together in specialist groups, with financial firms located around Milan and those linked to the automobile industry around Turin.

Northern Italy has a wide range of industries, and this diversity will ensure that it continues to provide much of Italy's employment. Italy is known for excellent design and this, combined with a skilled workforce and good trade links, should ensure that the region continues to be a powerhouse for employment and production.

The Galleria, a huge shopping mall in Milan, sells all the famous designer labels.

CASE STUDY
UBIEST – TREVISO

UbiEst is a high-tech firm located in Treviso. It specializes in gathering high-quality geographical map data, which it then organizes into different formats for its customers. These maps can show whatever the customer wants, such as monuments or shops of a certain type. It is a small, specialist company and typical of firms found in the northern region.

THE MEZZOGIORNO

There continues to be a large gap in employment and income levels between the north and south of Italy. The south has lagged behind the north in development, having fewer resources. Deforestation occurred early in the region's history and allowed soil erosion to take place over hundreds of years. The soils of the region today are generally poor and thin. By the middle of the twentieth century, the *Mezzogiorno* region was falling ever further behind the north in terms of development. Transport links were poor and land ownership was in the hands of a few wealthy families.

In 1950, the Italian government created an organization called the *Cassa per il Mezzogiorno* in order to improve agriculture and transport links in the area and try to develop a modern industrial base. Over the 34 years of its existence the *Cassa* did improve agricultural methods and production by

AVERAGE UNEMPLOYMENT RATE BY REGION (%) 2001	
Northwest	7.3
Northeast	4.8
Central (including Rome)	7.9
South (including Sicily and Sardinia)	20.4
ITALY AS A WHOLE	9.5

breaking up the large estates into individual farms. A new highway was built, linking the south to the north, and state-financed industry was set up in a triangle created by the three cities of Taranto, Brindisi and Bari. These industries were meant to attract others into the region. The quality of life did improve for southern Italians, but generally the gap between the regions did not get smaller.

Romanian workers pick vegetables by hand on an organic farm in Lazio. Organic farming is very labor intensive.

Further government support since 1984 has still not put an end to the differences in income and employment levels. The north has attracted young people from the south and there has been continual migration from the rural areas of southern Italy to the factories of the north. Unemployment is still high in the south, with youth unemployment being particularly high. Nationally the youth unemployment rate is 28 percent, but in many of the southern regions it tops 50 percent.

Since the 1990s there has been a change in the way help was given to the south. Large direct payments given in the past to the region do not seem to have resulted in much improvement. Now financial help, along with expert advice, is being targeted at specific projects and there must be some input from the local community or private investment.

In agricultural areas funding is available for farmers who wish to convert their holdings to organic farming, because the market for organic produce is growing. Italy has more than a quarter of the European Union's organic farming, growing organic animal feed, cereals and olives. Much of this funding has been in the south.

As the older heavy industries that were brought into the area by state funding become less profitable, it is important that other

Steelworks such as this one in Taranto were introduced by the government to help improve the economy of the south, but without success.

industries take their place. Developing the region's tourism potential is seen as an important method of generating revenue. Funding and training are available to help people set up, for example, small guest houses in areas such as Bari. The future for the south lies in diversifying its industries and giving its young people a reason to stay in the *Mezzogiorno*.

CASE STUDY
THE TARI PROJECT

Italy is a world leader in jewelry production and there is a well-established jewelry quarter in Naples. Although the old part of the city is the ideal location for jewelry shops, it is too cramped for manufacturing. Funding was given to develop a Jewelry Center with exhibition space outside the city. The site had good road, rail and air links. Training workshops and a research facility have also been added. Jobs at the center have increased 200 percent since it was created.

TRADE AND TRANSNATIONAL COMPANIES

Italy has the seventh-largest economy in the world, but its growth is slowing down. It is estimated that only 60 percent of Italians of working age are actually employed, and unemployment is an increasing problem.

One of the strengths of the Italian manufacturing industry is its attention to design and detail. This care for design is found in the many small, specialized firms that are typical of Italian industry. These firms are often family run, operating alongside similar enterprises in order to share expertise.

Globally there is a move toward transnational companies (TNCs). These are large companies with factories in more than one country that trade worldwide. Of the top 100 TNCs, 43 are found in the EU, but few are located in Italy. People associate good design with Italian manufacturing industry and are willing to pay for that expertise. Smaller companies tend to be more innovative and TNCs often buy in their expertise.

Hundreds of containers packed with a huge variety of goods are lined up for export at the docks of Palermo, Sicily.

CASE STUDY
BENETTON SUCCESS STORY

Benetton began in 1955 as a small, family-run clothing firm in Treviso, northern Italy. The company sold good-quality, well-designed sweaters door-to-door. Later, the firm sold its products to independently owned shops under the Benetton name. Today, there are 7,000 shops worldwide, with the majority in Europe. Benetton owns the 50 most important flagship stores in major cities such as Paris, New York, Osaka and Lisbon. About 3,500 people are directly employed by Benetton, and more than 50,000 are employed by its subcontractors. Up to 80 percent of its clothing production still takes place in Italy, produced by subcontractors such as Bronte Jeans in Sicily. There have been some problems with subcontractors in countries such as Turkey, where it is alleged that child labor has been employed. The company's magazine *Colors* reinforces its commitment to issues of global concern such as world hunger and is published in six languages in 80 countries. Recently, the company has diversified away from its core clothing business into running highway gas stations and toll roads.

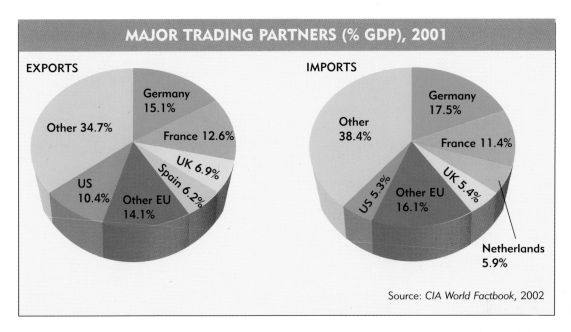

MAJOR TRADING PARTNERS (% GDP), 2001

EXPORTS

- Germany 15.1%
- France 12.6%
- UK 6.9%
- Spain 6.2%
- Other EU 14.1%
- US 10.4%
- Other 34.7%

IMPORTS

- Germany 17.5%
- France 11.4%
- UK 5.4%
- Netherlands 5.9%
- Other EU 16.1%
- US 5.3%
- Other 38.4%

Source: *CIA World Factbook*, 2002

CASE STUDY
FIAT

Fiat cars ready for export. Fiat is fighting to maintain its share of the European market.

Fiat, Italy's largest employer, was founded in Turin in 1899. Initially the company employed 150 workers. Today Fiat employs 221,000 worldwide in 60 countries. Although best known for car manufacturing, Fiat has diversified into truck and tractor production, publishing, insurance, metallurgy, aviation, robotics and manufacture of lubricants. Its car division now includes Fiat, Alfa Romeo, Lancia, Ferrari and Maserati. These cars are either produced by Fiat itself or under license in countries such as Italy, Brazil, Argentina, Morocco, China and India.

Recently the company has fallen behind foreign competition, and its market share within Europe has dropped from 14 percent in 1991 to less than 7 percent in 2003. In October 2002, 7,600 Italian autoworkers were laid off and most of the Fiat factories were operating only 75 percent of the time. Some of Fiat's factories are in the south of the country, and if these close there is very little other employment. The company has debts as a result of buying other companies in order to diversify and must now decide whether to continue as a car manufacturer within a larger organization such as General Motors or to sell off the car division and concentrate on its other interests.

EU and Italian flags fly together outside the Senate in Rome.

Today Italy is a republic, but the country has had few periods of political stability. Since 1945 Italy has had 59 changes of government – there have been nine changes since 1993! Italy has one of the world's largest economies. The country contributes to and participates in a broad range of international organizations.

THE UNITED NATIONS

Italy joined the United Nations (UN) in 1955 and is the fifth-largest contributor. It participates in peace-keeping in the trouble spots of the world, giving economic and humanitarian aid to less economically developed countries and also helping with the promotion of development. Italy is also the top contributor to the UN program against organized crime and promoted the formation of the International Criminal Court of Justice, which is part of a worldwide fight against international crime groups such as the Mafia (see page 47). Italy has 10,000 troops working on UN peace-keeping missions in areas such as Kosovo and Somalia.

THE EUROPEAN UNION

Italy was a founding member of the European Union (EU), whose aims include expanding economic and social progress, establishing European citizenship, ensuring freedom and security, and promoting Europe throughout the world.

Although Italy is a major contributor to the EU, the country also derives many benefits from its membership. Italy has benefited from EU funding for its problem areas, mainly in the *Mezzogiorno* region and the southern islands. The development of organic farming in Sicily (see page 29) came about largely because of EU funding, which supports farmers while they set up their organic farms and helps to improve irrigation. Many other areas get funding under the Less Favored Areas (LFA) programs. In mountainous regions where farms are small and unprofitable, for example, grants are given to encourage young farmers to stay on the land and maintain it. To have access to the grants they must follow environmentally friendly farming methods such as crop rotation and tree planting. Cities also benefit from funding by the EU. Palermo, in Sicily, has received money to help develop a sustainable public transport system.

The naval base at Spezia is an important base for NATO ships.

ITALY'S MEMBERSHIP OF ORGANIZATIONS

Italy belongs to the following international organizations:

EU European Union. In January 2004 there were 15 member countries of this economic union, with 10 others scheduled to join in May 2004.

UN United Nations. This group works to maintain peace and encourage development. There are 191 member countries

G8 The Group of 8. These more economically developed countries promote international trade and relations with less economically developed countries.

WEU Western European Union. This is an economic grouping of 10 countries. It was set up originally to form a defensive league but now aims to integrate other more easterly countries of Europe into a larger alliance.

WTO World Trade Organization. This organization governs rules of trade between nations. There are 146 members.

NATO North Atlantic Treaty Organization. This is a group of 19 member countries that work together to provide collective defense and security.

OECD Organization for Economic Cooperation and Development. A group of 30 members committed to the market economy and democratic government.

OSCE Organization for Security and Cooperation in Europe. This group is made up of 55 nations involved in security-related issues such as arms control.

TRANSPORT

Italy depends on good transport links to allow goods and people to reach their destinations. Northern Italy has a complex system of rail and road networks, but transport systems are not as well developed in the south. In the past the difference was even more pronounced until large amounts of government aid were made available from the late 1950s onward to help build up the region's transport routes.

ON THE ROADS

Italy has 6,450km of highway, leading from the Alpine tunnels and passes in the north to a hub around Milan. From here they radiate out to the coasts, and there are two main highway links to the south. The most important is the *Autostrada del Sol* (Highway to the Sun), which runs all the way down to the "toe" of Italy.

Italians have one of the highest levels of car ownership in the world, with more than 32 million on the road. Italians are known for their individuality and love of speed, but unfortunately this results in a road death toll nearly twice that of the United Kingdom, a country with a similar-sized landmass and population. Small cars dominate the Italian market because they are much easier to park than larger cars in Italy's congested city centers.

A new stretch of *autostrada* (highway), in Sicily. Such transport links may help improve the economy of southern Italy.

These girls will be able to beat the traffic on their Italian-built scooter.

CASE STUDY
FERRARA – A CITY FOR CYCLISTS

The city of Ferrara is located on the flat Po plain, which is ideal for cyclists. It is part of the Cities for Cyclists Network and does everything to encourage the use of bicycles. Although car ownership is high, many people in Ferrara drive to work and then use a bicycle for shopping or going out for lunch. About 90 percent of the population uses a bicycle at some time. Ferrara has created many cycle tracks to access as much of the city as possible, including a track that goes around the city walls. In some hotels in Ferrara, the price per room includes the use of a bike!

This high-speed train in the central station of Rome is about to depart for Milan.

RAILWAYS

Italy has 16,000km of railways. There are high-speed links between Rome, Florence and Milan. Several cities have metro lines (underground railways), including Genoa, Milan and Rome.

TRANSPORT BY AIR AND SEA

The national airline is Alitalia, which is 89 percent state owned. Like most airlines today, Alitalia is suffering from a downturn in air traffic since the terrorist attacks in New York in 2001. Italy has 17 main commercial airports. The busiest is in Rome, with nearly 26 million passengers passing through each year.

Italy has a large merchant fleet and many ports, the most important being those of Genoa on the Mediterranean Sea, Trieste on the Adriatic Sea and Augusta in Sicily.

TRANSPORT NETWORKS

Main roads
...... Railways
✈ International airports
⚓ Ports

LIECHTENSTEIN
SWITZERLAND
FRANCE
SLOVENIA
Trieste
Turin   Milan   Verona   Venice
Ferrara
Genoa   Bologna   CROATIA
SAN MARINO
Pisa   Florence
LIGURIAN SEA
ADRIATIC SEA
N
CORSICA (FRANCE)
Rome
Bari
Naples   Brindisi
Taranto
SARDINIA
TYRRHENIAN SEA
Cagliari
MEDITERRANEAN SEA
Palermo   Messina
SICILY   Catania

0   200km
0   100 miles

CASE STUDY
INTEGRATED TRANSPORT IN GENOA

The port city of Genoa developed a new urban transport plan in 2000 with the aims of encouraging more use of public transport and developing better links between bus, car and rail systems. In 2002 it was estimated that nearly 50 percent of daily traffic movements within the city were made by local public transport.

Features of Genoa's integrated transport system include the following:

- Buses have satellite systems that enable them to transmit and relay their positions to screens at bus stops to keep passengers informed.

- Priority lanes are provided for buses.

- Rail and bus timetables are linked.

- An electric bus connects the "park and ride" areas to the city center.

- There are toll charges for cars to enter the city center.

URBAN ITALY

Italy has a long history of urbanization, with cities such as Rome and Florence existing from before the Roman Empire. During the Middle Ages many of the cities became independent city-states under the influence of powerful families such as the Medici of Florence. Their wealth grew mainly by trade, and Italy became one of the most cultured regions in Europe. From the sixteenth century Italy's powerful cities declined in power as other countries such as Spain and Austria took control of Italian lands.

After the unification of Italy in 1861, Rome became the capital. Since that time there has been much rural-urban migration to cities, especially from the impoverished farmlands of the south. Today these cities have to cope with the problems of modern urban living, often with historic city centers that must be preserved and protected. Italy does not want to stay in the past, and there have been many urban initiatives to improve the quality of life for city residents while preserving a city's historical heritage.

ROME

Known as the Eternal City, Rome has an urban history of more than 2,000 years. It was built near a major crossing point of the Tiber River on seven low hills overlooking the floodplain. Today the city is a mixture of expanding modern suburbs with ancient buildings at its core. Service industries such as local government and tourism employ 82 percent of Rome's working population. Rome's manufacturing industry tends to focus on small specialist firms in fashion accessories and, more recently, high-tech industry including software design and aerospace.

The city has many problems arising from its growth. One of the most obvious is traffic congestion. Most of its service industry is based in the city center. Because most of the population lives in the suburbs, this means huge daily flows of people and cars. At its historic center the city has many narrow streets, which are not suited to today's motor traffic. With a lack of off-road parking areas,

TELECOMMUNICATIONS DATA

Mainline Phones	25,000,000
Mobile Phones	20,500,000
Internet Service Providers	93

Source: *CIA World Factbook*, 2002

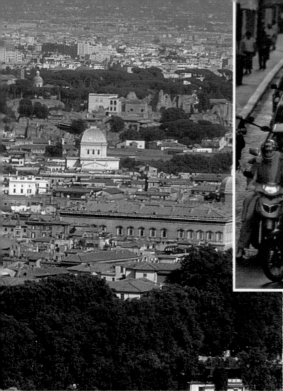

ABOVE: A busy intersection in Rome. All of Italy's major cities have traffic congestion.
LEFT: Rome's cityscape provides a view of ancient, historical monuments standing alongside modern buildings.

the congestion is made worse by people parking cars on the streets, thus making them even narrower.

To reduce traffic, public transport needs to be improved. The metro system covers only limited parts of the city and is not coping with increasing numbers of passengers. However, planned improvements are under way. Most buses, with the exception of the electric ones in Rome's center, are highly polluting but are well used. In 2000, Rome's ageing tram system got a boost when the city ordered 28 new trams with the aim of getting more commuters out of their cars and into public transport. Experiments have been carried out with telecommuting, so that some local government employees can work from home, reducing car traffic in the center.

Many of Rome's high-rise apartment buildings are cramped and shoddily built, leading to a poor quality of life for those who live there.

SOCIAL PROBLEMS

A housing shortage in Rome sparked construction in the 1960s and 1970s, but the poor-quality high-rise apartment buildings that resulted are now rife with social problems. These areas have high unemployment levels. Many of the inhabitants are immigrants, so there is also racial tension. Graffiti is common throughout these housing projects, but now it is found even on the ancient monuments of the historic center. The city government has set up an Office of City Decorum to try and clean up buildings and to change youth behavior.

MILAN

Milan is the economic capital of Italy and has a wide range of industries both in manufacturing (such as engineering and textiles) and in services, especially finance, design, publishing, and research and development. It is the hub of the road and rail network in northern Italy and an important commercial center, home to the world's first shopping mall – the *Galleria Vittorio Emmanuel,* begun in 1865!

With industrial suburbs and heavy traffic, the city suffers from severe air pollution. Several times in 2002 the pollution levels were five times the permitted maximum. Cars were banned from the city on Sundays and people were encouraged to use the trams in an effort to reduce the pollution.

Many people are moving away from the city to live in more rural areas, and the remaining population is ageing. About 6 percent are over age 75, and in the decaying northern part of the city 27 percent are older than 65. In order to support this increasingly dependent population the city has begun a project to convert derelict buildings into service centers for the elderly. These include a day center and a unit to help the elderly remain independent.

GENOA

Genoa is an important port in the north of Italy. Toward the end of the twentieth century, port activity declined as Italy's industries became more service based. Port-based industries closed and the city's unemployment figures rose. Genoa is a culturally mixed city, and there were increasing racial tensions and a rising crime rate in the deprived areas next to the port.

LEFT: Creation of pedestrian-only zones in central Milan has helped to reduce air pollution.
BELOW: Milan is Italy's financial capital.

Genoa's new skyline is dominated by a unique mast sculpture by artist Renzo Piano.

In 1992 the Old Port area was renovated. A world-class aquarium was built and the port buildings were converted into bars and restaurants to attract tourists.

Money from the EU was later used to bring new life to the rundown historic center by developing the Urban Observatory (a research and information center) in a restored convent and an urban studies facility in a redundant church. These projects have improved the area and encouraged other developments. The EU named Genoa Europe's City of Culture for 2004. The city plans to further regenerate its harbor area and link it to the restored historic center.

NAPLES

Naples was once an important port in the south of Italy. Although one of the poorest cities in the EU, it is still the most important city in the *Mezzogiorno* region. Its heavy industries, set up by the Italian government, have mainly closed, leaving the area with high unemployment, often over 50 percent.

Corruption and the siphoning of money by the Mafia (a criminal organization; see page 47) has meant that many redevelopment projects did not get started, and many of those that did were not completed. A new mayor started a new phase of redevelopment in the mid-1990s. Work has focused on the port and central areas because it is hoped

that improvements there will stimulate tourism and therefore create more jobs. An increased police presence on the streets led to a huge drop in crime, and tourism grew by 40 percent as visitors began to feel safe in the city. Many museums and palaces have now been restored and opened to the public. The main square has been paved and closed to traffic, acting as a vibrant, pedestrian-friendly core to the area.

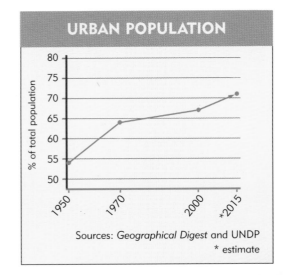

URBAN POPULATION

% of total population vs. years (1950, 1970, 2000, *2015)

Sources: *Geographical Digest* and UNDP
* estimate

A dramatic sky over the Bay of Naples.

Italy's population structure is changing. In about 30 years' time, most people will be more than 60 years old.

Italy has a population of nearly 58 million, but the country is now at a stage where its death rate is higher than its birth rate. This means that without immigration Italy's population will decline.

Life expectancy is increasing, with women expected to live to 82 years and men to 76. In 1960 there were about 5 million people over 65. In 2000 the population exceeded 11 million, forming nearly 19 percent of the total population. In contrast children aged 0–14 years now form only 14 percent of the population. This means that in the future there will be fewer people of working age to support an increasing number of the elderly.

INTERNATIONAL EMIGRATION

During the nineteenth and twentieth centuries many Italians emigrated to find a better life in other European countries, the United States,

MIGRATION WITHIN ITALY

For much of the twentieth century, Italians in the south were attracted to the more affluent northern region, a movement that continues today although in far smaller numbers.

PUSH FROM THE SOUTH	PULL TO THE NORTH
High unemployment levels	Range of manufacturing/ service jobs
Very small unprofitable farms	Perceived better lifestyle
Poor soil and soil erosion	Jobs with regular wage rather than seasonal agricultural jobs
Lack of job opportunities other than farming	Higher wages

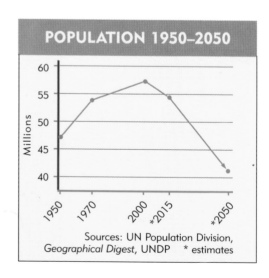

POPULATION 1950–2050

Millions

60
55
50
45
40

1950 1970 2000 *2015 *2050

Sources: UN Population Division, *Geographical Digest*, UNDP   * estimates

South America, Canada and Australia. Parts of many foreign cities such as Boston, have "Little Italy" districts. In some cases almost all the young people from a village would emigrate after hearing about how others were making a new life for themselves. It is thought that more than 26 million Italians emigrated, largely from the depressed southern region. Since the 1970s, as Italy has grown wealthier, this movement has largely stopped.

INTERNATIONAL IMMIGRATION

Italy's peninsula has a very long coastline, which makes it vulnerable to illegal immigration, especially from Albania and the countries of North Africa. Italy receives 15 percent of all of the EU's international immigrants. In 1999, 2 percent of its population was foreign, mainly from Morocco and Albania. Most of the migrants are unskilled and find work in the agricultural, construction and tourism industries. Often these are jobs that Italians do not want to do, but recently Italy has drafted some much stricter immigration laws to try to stem the flow of illegal immigrants. In future it is likely that there will be laws limiting employment prospects for immigrants in order to try to deter the purely economic migrants (people who migrate simply to obtain a better lifestyle).

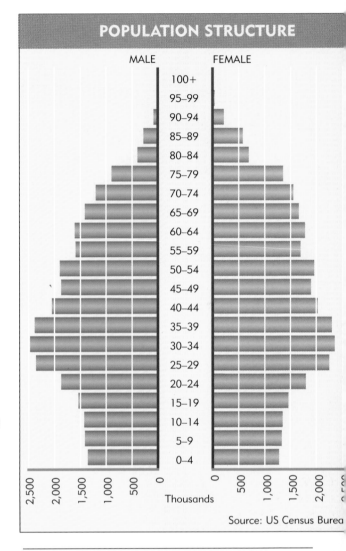

POPULATION STRUCTURE

MALE FEMALE

Age groups: 100+, 95–99, 90–94, 85–89, 80–84, 75–79, 70–74, 65–69, 60–64, 55–59, 50–54, 45–49, 40–44, 35–39, 30–34, 25–29, 20–24, 15–19, 10–14, 5–9, 0–4

Male scale: 2,500, 2,000, 1,500, 1,000, 500, 0

Thousands

Female scale: 0, 500, 1,000, 1,500, 2,000

Source: US Census Bureau

African migrants selling crafts on the streets.

ECONOMIC MIGRANTS

Italy has always offered asylum to people with a genuine fear of persecution in their home countries, but it is beginning to be swamped by economic migrants. In 1999 Italy received 33,360 asylum applications, including 1,800 from Kosovo and 1,015 from Bosnia.

Girl scouts in Abruzzo. In Italy many scout groups include boys and girls.

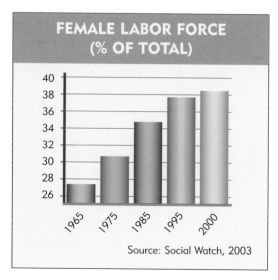

FEMALE LABOR FORCE (% OF TOTAL)

Source: Social Watch, 2003

MARRIAGE AND FAMILY LIFE

On average, Italians get married at the age of 28, and 75 percent of people still marry in church. Italy's divorce rate is one of the lowest in Europe at 7 percent (compared with 48 percent in the United States). Women are now much more likely to work outside the home, and many decide not to have children or to delay when they have them. Italians love children, but today they are having fewer, with each woman on average producing 1.2 babies. This means that the birth rate has fallen below population replacement level.

Family is very important to Italians and much of their social life revolves around the extended family, including grandparents and cousins. Once a baby is born, both parents can have three months at home on full pay.

Childcare is both expensive and difficult to find, so grandparents often step in to look after children while the parents are at work. Although church attendance is falling in Italy, 95 percent of babies are still baptized into the Roman Catholic Church.

EDUCATION

At the age of six, all children begin at primary school, and they start to learn a foreign language, usually English, by the age of seven. Secondary school is divided into two stages – the first is from the ages of 11 to 14. Then children have a choice of schools from 14 to 18.

Rome's La Sapienza University is the largest in Italy.

In Italy people are living longer and having fewer children. In the future there will be more old people than young ones.

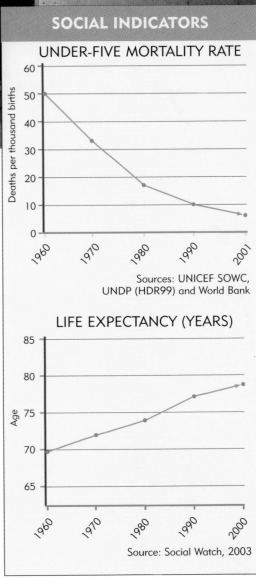

UNDER-FIVE MORTALITY RATE

Deaths per thousand births

60
50
40
30
20
10
0

1960 1970 1980 1990 2001

Sources: UNICEF SOWC, UNDP (HDR99) and World Bank

LIFE EXPECTANCY (YEARS)

Age

85
80
75
70
65

1960 1970 1980 1990 2000

Source: Social Watch, 2003

Many choose technical schools, which concentrate on administration, commerce and industrial practice. Other options include vocational schools, where students study a craft, such as carpentry or jewelry design, and the more academic options of the classics, language or science schools. On completing their studies at 18, students leave with a diploma, which means they can go on to university.

Unemployment is high among young people across much of Italy, so qualifications are essential for getting any sort of job. Most young Italians live at home, largely because of cost, although some mothers do not want to let their sons go. Young Italians therefore do not have a lot of privacy, and many regard cars as something they must have in order to gain a bit of private space and the means of escape!

At 18 many young people progress to university, often in the nearest town so that they can live at home. Italy has 47 universities. Rome's La Sapienza is the largest, with 170,000 students. The lecture halls are usually crowded, and students are lucky to get a seat.

HEALTH CARE

Italy has a good level of health care but this will be strained as the population ages. Italians live longer than almost any other nationality in Europe, and they can expect to draw a pension

at 56 or after working for 35 years. This will soon change because more people are living longer. In order for everyone to have a pension it must be taken at a later age. Late in their lives, the elderly are usually looked after by their families. Italians see it as a failure of the family if a parent has to move into a retirement home, but this may become more common as children move away in search of jobs.

ITALIANS AND LEISURE

Italian leisure time mainly revolves around home and family, and 60 percent of Italians spend two hours a day meeting friends and relatives. It is traditional in Italy, especially in the summer, for the family to go out together after the evening meal to walk up and down the local streets. Here they meet and talk to friends and local people to see what is going on in the area and to gossip. This evening parading is known as *la passeggiata* (which means "the walk"). The squares in towns are often buzzing late into the evening. Families may stop at a café for drinks of beer and coffee as part of *la passeggiata*. The children may have a granita, a drink made from fresh fruit juice and crushed ice.

Visitors to Gran Paradiso National Park cool off by a lake.

Television viewing is very popular and 99 percent of homes own at least one TV. Most Italians watch at least two hours of TV per day. RAI is the state-owned television company, and it has three stations, which offer the best-quality programs.

There is no truly national newspaper, but *La Repubblica* of Rome and the *Corriere della Sera* of Milan do cover some national issues. More than half of the population reads a newspaper at least once a week.

Film viewing remains popular, despite the ownership of video recorders and DVD players. Most large towns have several

La passeggiata: People enjoy the nightlife at a restaurant in Lucca.

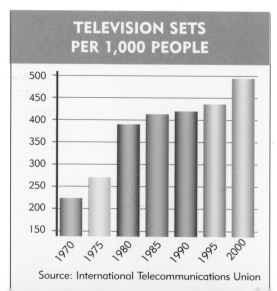

TELEVISION SETS PER 1,000 PEOPLE

Source: International Telecommunications Union

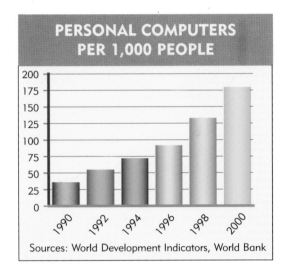

PERSONAL COMPUTERS PER 1,000 PEOPLE

Sources: World Development Indicators, World Bank

SPORTS

Italians are passionate about soccer, and it is the national sport. There are three leagues, with Serie A being the top division. Top teams include AC Milan, Inter Milan and Juventus.

There is now a growing interest in rugby, and in 2000 Italy joined Ireland, Wales, Scotland, England and France to form the Six Nations Championship.

Auto racing is another popular spectator sport. Italy has two Grand Prix racing circuits – the Imola Circuit in San Marino and the Monza Circuit near Milan.

Hunting is also popular and there are more than 800,000 regular hunters in Italy. They shoot rabbits, wild boar and, more controversially, songbirds, which are protected in many other countries.

theaters or a multiscreen theater. The Venice Film Festival, founded in 1932, is the oldest in the world.

Italians enjoy all kinds of music but are perhaps most associated with opera. The world-famous tenor Luciano Pavarotti has done much to give Italian opera a high profile. There are many opera venues in Italy, including ones held in the open air such as at Verona. La Scala, in Milan, is the most famous opera house in Italy.

VACATIONS

In 1997, 52 percent of Italians had spent their vacations away from home, although three quarters had spent their time off within Italy. For travel abroad, France is the most popular destination, followed by Spain. Many Italians enjoy camping, and there are more than 2,000 campsites in Italy, ranging from very rustic sites to to ones that offer swimming pools, saunas and restaurants.

Hiking is an increasingly popular activity in Italy, and there are plenty of marked trails for visitors to follow.

ISLAND LIFE

Italy is largely a peninsula of southern
Europe but it also has many islands within
its territory, the largest of which are Sicily
and Sardinia.

AEOLIAN ISLANDS

North of Sicily are the Aeolian islands, a group
of volcanoes. One of them is Vulcano, which
gave its name to all other volcanoes, but
today it just rumbles and smokes. Visitors
often go there for the famous hot mud baths.
Lipari is the largest of the Aeolian islands and
is the center for ferries to and from the other
islands in the group. One of its main products
is pumice stone, for use in the home and as an
industrial abrasive. Stromboli is the most
isolated of the islands and is home to the
world's most continuously active volcano. It
still erupts about every 20 minutes and is
a spectacular sight at night. Due to the
island's isolation before the ferry and
hydrofoil connections were made, many

people left the island and emigrated to
Australia in search of work and a better life.
Stromboli has a population of 500. Because of
its isolation, lack of space for development
and its quite rainy climate, it does not attract
mass tourism. Most people who visit this
island do so to walk up the flanks of the
volcano and look down into its fiery heart.

SICILY

Sicily is one of the most densely populated
areas of Italy, having a total population of
5 million. The island has been ruled by Greeks,
Romans, Arabs, Norman French and Spanish.
The Sicilian accent still has an Arab influence
and the people can trace their ancestors to
a wide variety of nationalities. For many
inhabitants of the island, they are Sicilian
first and Italian second. Sicily is closer

Stromboli's traditional fishing industry
continues alongside the island's increasingly
important tourist industry.

geographically to Africa than to Milan, and it is in a good position within the Mediterranean basin to have easy links with North African countries. There is only limited industry and very poor road and rail networks hinder commerce and travel in the island.

Industries already established there include textile industries and food processing. Sicily grows and exports citrus fruit, especially lemons, as well as a range of other agricultural produce. It relies heavily on irrigation, but there are problems with the water supply due to government money meant for improvement going into the pockets of the Mafia (see box).

Plans are under way to build a bridge across the Strait of Messina to join Sicily with the mainland in order to speed up traffic links. It would be 5km long and would cost up to $5.3 billion. Sicilians are saying it might be better to first improve the roads, railways and water supplies on the island before carrying out these plans. They are not sure they want to be permanently linked to Italy.

THE MAFIA

Sicily has very high unemployment levels, and much of the money that has been provided by the EU or the Italian government has not found its way to the planned projects, partly because of the Mafia, a criminal organization. The Mafia is involved in drug trafficking, prostitution, demanding money for protection for businesses and diverting government money into their own funds. Recently much has been done to try to reduce its influence by arresting and taking its leaders to court. People are now more confident and are speaking out against the organization. It is hoped that international companies will then want to locate on the island.

A fruit stall in Palermo. Sicily's warm climate means that a wide range of fruit can be grown.

TOURISM

Italy has had a long history of tourism, dating back to the days of the Roman Empire, when officials running the empire would go to Rome for a business trip or to the country to rest and recuperate. In the eighteenth and nineteenth centuries Italy was one of the countries in the Grand Tour, a tour of Europe undertaken by aristocratic young people as part of their education. Today, Italy is an important destination for tourists, both within and beyond Europe.

Italy has a varied landscape, ranging from the snowy peaks of the Alps to the rocky coastline of Liguria. Tourists flock to visit the arid landscapes of the south, the sandy beaches on the Adriatic Sea and Italy's volcanoes, including Mount Etna. Popular tourist destinations include the great cities such as Venice for its canals, Florence for its art and architecture, and Rome for the Vatican City and the Colosseum. Archaeology is a tourist magnet, with historic sites such as Pompeii (destroyed by the eruption of Vesuvius in A.D. 79) attracting 2.3 million visitors a year.

The stunning scenery of Monte Bianco attracts visitors during the winter and summer months.

NUMBERS OF TOURISTS, 2003	
France	66,800,000
United States	50,000,000
Spain	43,500,000
Italy	35,000,000
United Kingdom	26,000,000

Source: Worldworx

For visitors to Lazio, the beautiful beaches are the top attractions.

Tourism is the main source of income for cities such as Venice, although the city is sometimes in danger of being swamped by the huge numbers of visitors. In the height of summer the streets are so crowded that there is little of the magical experience that earlier travelers spoke of. The present Italian government realizes that tourism is one of Italy's most important industries and is funding many projects to try to improve tourism income. This is especially true in the *Mezzogiorno*, where tourism is seen as an alternative to the dying heavy industry of the Bari-Brindisi-Taranto area.

CASE STUDY
FLORENCE

The Ponte Vecchio is one of Florence's most visited sites.

The city of Florence flourished in the fifteenth century and was a center of the Renaissance. Most of the buildings from this period are still in existence, and this is what makes Florence so attractive to visitors. The historic center, with its beautiful buildings filled with artwork such as Michelangelo's David, now attracts 7 million tourists a year.

The huge numbers of tourists have created many problems for the city. Chewing gum is trodden into the marble floors. Crowds gather around statues in museums and in the street, touching and climbing on them. The acid in human sweat eats away at the marble. The whole of the center of Florence is of historical interest, and in 1982 it was designated a World Heritage Site. However, this was not enough to protect the city, and in the early 1990s the city council decided to draw up a Code of Conduct, which is given out to all tourists in the city to help them protect and appreciate its beauty. Tourist Police are employed to keep an eye on unruly behavior.

In the 1980s, the Uffizi, Italy's most important art gallery, had up to 11,000 visitors a day! Today, the daily number of visitors is limited to 5,000. The city council is considering charging entry fees to the historic city to pay for its maintenance and restoration.

Gran Paradiso was one of Italy's first national parks, protecting high Alpine mountains and valleys.

During the twentieth century, Italy became aware that its landscapes and wildlife were under threat from clearance for agriculture and urbanization. In 1922, Italy's first national park was established in the Apennines, the Abruzzo National Park. Today, 10 percent of Italy is under state protection and 5 percent of the land has national park status. Italy's regional and national parks attract more than 17 million visitors per year, and some are now having excessive visitor traffic in the summer.

MAIN NATIONAL PARKS

LIECHTENSTEIN   A U S T R I A
SWITZERLAND   Stelvio
N
SLOVENIA
Dolomiti
Bellunesi
Gran
Paradiso   CROATIA
SAN
MARINO   BOSNIA -
HERZEGOVINA
Foreste
Casentinesi

CORSICA   Maiella
(FRANCE)   Abruzzo
Gargano

SARDINIA

Capo
Rizzuto
Aspromonte
SICILY
0   200km
0   100 miles

● National parks
● Marine reserve

Italy is now protecting many of its wild coastal areas, such as in the marine reserve of Circeo National Park, Lazio.

Horseback riding is just one of many activities available in Abruzzo National Park.

Situated just two hours' drive away from Rome, Abruzzo National Park is one of the most visited in Italy. It is the oldest and the largest of the parks, covering 50,000 hectares of mountain peaks, rivers, lakes and forest. It contains 45 percent of Italy's species of mammals and more than 2,000 different plant species. The animals include the "big seven" – bear, wolf, chamois, red deer, roe deer, eagle and lynx – which receive full protection within the park.

To improve the balance between protecting the animals and allowing public access, in the 1980s park authorities divided the park into four zones. The first is a core zone, where there is no human activity and the wildlife is left totally alone. The second zone is the General Reserve, which can be accessed with a permit. The third is the Protection Zone, where people can visit and enjoy the landscape and walking trails. This acts as a buffer to the fourth zone, the Development Zone, where hotels and restaurants can be located, and where some limited extraction of resources such as trees is allowed. Even here all development is small scale and there are no large hotels or ski lifts.

National parks tend to cover large areas and aim to protect and conserve landscapes and the wildlife within. They also promote access for recreation, which can conflict with conservationist aims. A certain amount of economic activity takes place within the parks, but this is carefully monitored and inappropriate development is not allowed. Education is important, and the national parks have 131 visitor centers and 35 environmental educational centers.

Reserves tend to be small and usually exist to protect a particular species or a threatened landscape. Ramsar wetlands are wetland areas of worldwide importance and include salt marshes, estuaries and bogs. (Ramsar was the Turkish town where the idea of international protection for wetlands was first put forward at a conference.)

Capo Rizzuto Marine Reserve is a 36-km stretch of coastline along the "toe" of Italy, in the region of Calabria. It consists of eight headlands beyond which is a series of underwater terraces covered with rare marine plant and animal communities. There are small reefs and areas covered with seaweed known as "submerged prairies." Here there are sponges, a wide variety of fish, and dolphins. No fishing or water sports are allowed in the immediate area. Visitors can snorkel or travel in glass-bottomed boats to see the rich biodiversity of these waters. Nearby, an aquarium contains specimens of the species found in the reserve.

PROTECTED AREAS IN ITALY

National parks	*20
National reserves	150
Regional parks	89
Regional reserves	270
Ramsar wetland sites	47
Marine reserves	16

* 4 more currently being established

ENVIRONMENTAL PROBLEMS

Italians have become much more environmentally aware over the last decade. Air pollution has become more noticeable both in the quality of the air breathed and in the impact it is having on Italy's buildings. Ancient architecture that has survived for hundreds of years is now being eaten away by the chemicals in the air and dissolved in the acid rain. Nearly two-thirds of Italians are more worried about air pollution than any other environmental concern, perhaps because

Italian cities frequently suffer from smog caused by industrial fumes and vehicle exhaust gases.

IMPACTS OF ACID RAIN ON ITALY'S ALPINE FORESTS

Acid rain has damaged the forests in the Italian Alps. Known effects that can be attributed to acid rain are as follows:

- Trees have yellowing leaves and more leaves drop.

- Damage reduces the trees' resistance to disease and pests.

- Trees are more prone to being blown down because they are not healthy.

- If soil is very acidic, seedlings will not be able to establish.

- If large numbers of trees die, soil erosion occurs because slopes are exposed to the full force of the rain.

- With fewer trees, these areas are more prone to avalanches in winter.

CASE STUDY
AIR AND WATER POLLUTION IN MILAN

In an effort to reduce the levels of pollution in the city center, Milan became one of the first Italian cities to invest in a tram system.

Milan's numerous factories and power stations contribute to large amounts of pollution in the form of gases and particulates. The Po plain has a great deal of fog and still air, so the pollution is not easily blown away but hangs above the cities for days. Milan has run "Car-Free Sundays" regularly since 1999 to try to reduce the pollution. Sometimes a lack of rain can make the pollution worse because it

remains in the atmosphere, causing problems for asthma and bronchitis sufferers. At the beginning of 2002, the problem was so bad that Milan had to close the city center to cars for three days a week to clear the air.

Milan has invested in more trams and buses and has an electric car–sharing scheme. Drivers pay a membership fee and then use a magnetic card to access one of the electric cars at a number of locations. They pay for the distance traveled and return the car to another drop-off point. There are 500 of these electric cars, helping to reduce pollution in the city center.

Wastewater and sewage remain a problem. Milan's population is nearly 3 million, but all of its sewage goes untreated into the Lambro River, a tributary of the Po. This has caused eutrophication – a process that deprives water of needed oxygen – at the Po delta.

it is the one that affects most of them on a daily basis.

As part of the EU, Italy has signed the Kyoto Protocol, which states that the country will reduce its greenhouse gas emissions by 2008–2012 to 8 percent lower than the figure in 1990. By 2003, Italy had in fact increased its emissions of these gases! Part of the problem is the Italians' love of cars, as well as the fact that most of Italy's electricity still comes from the burning of fossil fuels. Legambiente, Italy's most important environmental group, is campaigning for a more sustainable way of life for the country, and there are branches in most large cities and towns.

CASE STUDY
ACID RAIN IN THE NORTH

Many of the industries and power stations of northern Italy produce sulfur dioxide, which can make rainfall much more acidic than normal. Added to Italy's own emissions, pollutants are carried to Italy in the winds from Germany, the Czech Republic and Slovakia. This has caused acidification of the lakes in the subalpine region such as Lake Como, and many of its lake organisms have been greatly reduced in number. The forests in the Italian Alps have also been badly affected.

TOURISM AND THE ENVIRONMENT

Tourism is causing problems in places such as Florence and Venice, where numbers of visitors are very high. Skiing in the winter months is also creating problems in the alpine environment. Mountain forests are cleared to make way for ski runs, and tree-felling results in reduced avalanche control, as well as making the areas less scenic. Mountains are scarred by the installation of ski lifts. Today the Italian Alps are an increasingly popular ski destination, but if the problems this tourism causes are not solved, Italy may well lose visitors as the environment is degraded.

HUNTING

Hunting is popular in Italy, and most of it is carried out legally. However, one sector that is often illegal is the hunting and trapping of birds. In the north, around Lake Garda, hunters catch songbirds and swallows using fine nylon nets, called mist nets, or spring traps. The trapped birds die a slow death. A survey carried out in 2000 found that 2,000 songbirds were trapped in the area, 80 percent of which were robins. Swallows are now protected, and several "farms for swallows" have been set up in Italy. One was

The more tourists there are, the more litter they bring with them, adding to mess on the streets.

opened in 2002 on a dairy farm in the Ticino Regional Park, near Milan, where the farmer uses fewer pesticides in his farming to encourage insects and therefore attract the swallows. The farm is used as an educational resource and a recreational area for people who wish to watch the birds.

HUNTING BIRDS OF PREY

Birds of prey such as the honey buzzard migrate to Europe from Africa and use the Strait of Messina, between Sicily and the mainland, as a route to Europe. Every year hunters wait to shoot them, and until recently 5,000 protected birds of prey were illegally shot each year. Increasing awareness of their importance and careful monitoring of the strait has meant that only a few hundred are now killed.

CASE STUDY
VENICE – A WATERY CITY

Founded more than 2,000 years ago, Venice is built on wooden pilings sunk into the waters of a lagoon on the Adriatic coast. It became a powerful city-state in the Middle Ages and attracted artists and architects, whose works are now visited by millions of tourists each year.

Flooding is a growing problem for the city. Water is taken from an aquifer (a layer of rock that holds water) beneath the city, and this is causing the lagoon bed to sink – 23cm over the last 100 years. Global warming is leading to an overall rise in sea levels, and there are more severe storms and tidal surges. Part of the main lagoon has had a deep channel dredged to allow large tankers to access the industrial port area. Wash from all the ships adds to the problem of water damage, and the building of concrete quays means that there is no open land to absorb any excess water, so the city continues to flood. In 2001, St Mark's Square flooded more than 90 times.

The solution is a controversial tidal barrier in 79 hinged moving sections, which will rise from the bed of the lagoon to protect the city whenever a really high tide is predicted. The scheme is called Project Moses. Environmentalists feel that what is needed is a more sustainable plan, including stopping the extraction of water from under the city, preventing further building around the lagoon and filling in the deep water channel, allowing only smaller vessels into the port. They argue that Venice is unique and should be preserved at all costs.

These buildings in Venice have been damaged by rising water levels. The problem is getting worse as the city suffers more frequent floods.

These new buildings in Naples reflect the city's move toward a more modern, varied economic base.

Italy has the seventh-strongest economy in the world, but can it maintain this? The 1992 Rio Earth Summit urged all nations to try to develop sustainable lifestyles. Italy has several problems to face in the twenty-first century, and decisions made in the next few years will impact on people and ecosystems for many years to come.

This polluted river in Lazio shows the impact of pouring untreated waste into watercourses.

Agriculture

Centuries of soil erosion, deforestation and overgrazing have led to poor farming landscapes. More money needs to be invested in keeping hill farmers on the land and to encourage young farmers to stay. Money needs to be made available to allow them to farm in a more environmentally friendly way, which will help preserve the traditional landscapes and yet support wildlife.

ENERGY RESOURCES

Italy is heavily dependent on the car, and there are severe problems of air pollution in all its major cities because of this. Keeping to the Kyoto agreement means that the country must reduce its greenhouse gas emissions. That can only be done by reducing the use of fossil fuels for both transport and electricity generation. The trams in Milan and Rome and the development of green transport policies in Palermo in Sicily show the way forward. More money is being invested in alternative energy sources, but Italy's emissions are still too high to meet the targets set by the Kyoto Protocol.

THE GRAYING POPULATION

Italy has an ageing population that will present serious challenges over the next 20–30 years. More services directed at the elderly must be set up, particularly because the tradition of caring for elderly parents at home may well break down under the pressures of modern living, with more women going out to work.

TOURISM

Italians are learning to treasure their past and may soon make tourists pay a price that includes payment for the damage they cause just by being in Italy. This is not only direct damage but includes tourists' contributions to city pollution by using a car or having arrived by air, each of which has an impact on greenhouse gases. In Florence, although fewer tourists are allowed into the Ufizzi (see page 49) there has not been a reduction in revenues and the collection is not put under as much strain.

IMMIGRATION

Considered a problem at the beginning of the twenty-first century, immigration may be a blessing later on because there are not enough young people working in Italy to support the growing population of elderly people or to fill the jobs of the future. Italy needs help from

Retirees enjoying the sun. Italy's huge pension bill must be reduced. This means younger people will have to work for longer than their parents to have a pension.

the EU to police its extensive coastal boundaries so that international migrants who wish to live in Italy do so legally and can be given suitable support to begin a new life.

BRIDGING THE DIVIDE

A young nation, Italy came into its own during the twentieth century and wishes to sustain its lifestyle into the twenty-first and beyond. However, the mismatch between the industrial north and the underdeveloped south throws into question the country's ability to maintain the status quo. Certain forces in the north want that region to become independent from the southern region, which they regard as a drain on their economy. That may be the greatest challenge for the future – ensuring that the south continues to develop and be a full partner within the country of Italy.

Acid rain Rainfall that is more acid than usual, caused by rainwater mixing with pollutants such as sulfur dioxide and nitrous oxides.

Alpine tundra A vegetation zone found high up mountains, beyond the timberline. Most of the vegetation includes mosses, lichens and low-growing grasses.

Altitude The measurement of height above sea level.

Aqueduct An artificial channel constructed to carry water.

Biodiversity The variety of species found within an area.

Coalition A grouping together of several organizations or political parties who then act as one.

Counterurbanization The movement of people away from urban centers to smaller villages and towns.

Deforestation Cutting down trees and not replanting them.

Delta A triangular-shaped landscape feature made up of sediments transported by a river and deposited at its mouth.

Desertification Creation of desertlike conditions in arid areas, usually by human actions such as overgrazing and deforestation.

Emigrant A person who leaves a country or region to live elsewhere.

European Union (EU) A group of countries that are working together financially, economically and socially.

Eutrophication The enrichment of freshwater by excess nutrients. This results in the growth of huge amounts of algae. When they die and decay most of the oxygen in the water is used up, and few living things can survive in it.

Floodplain The wide floor of a river valley, over which it may flood.

Fold mountains Mountains created by pressure within the Earth's crust, which causes layers of rock to slowly fold in on themselves and rise up.

Fossil fuel Fuels including coal, oil and gas made up of the fossilized remains of plants and microorganisms that lived millions of years ago.

Geothermal energy Energy extracted from water or steam heated by hot rocks below the Earth's surface.

Glacier A slow-moving river of ice found mainly in high mountains.

Gross Domestic Product (GDP) The total monetary value of goods and services produced by a country in a single year.

Gross National Income (GNI) Sometimes called the Gross National Product, or GNP, this is the total value of goods and services produced by a country, plus any earnings from overseas, in a single year.

High-tech industry Industry that uses the latest production techniques and technology such as computing and electronics.

Immigrant A person who comes to live in a new country or region.

Levee A raised bank that is formed naturally by a river, although humans may build them up higher as a form of flood protection.

Multipurpose forestry Forestry that provides space for recreation, conservation and education, as well as extracting timber.

Peninsula Land surrounded on three sides by water.

Photovoltaic cells Cells that can produce electrical power when sunlight falls on them; solar cells.

Plain A large area of flat land.

Plate A very large section of the Earth's crust composed of rock several kilometers thick, which moves slowly across the planet's surface.

Richter scale A measurement used to determine the intensity of an earthquake.

Service industry An industry that provides services to the public, such as transportation, tourism and communications.

Soil erosion The wearing away and transportation of the soil layer.

Surface runoff The overland movement of water after rainfall.

Telecommuting Working from home for a company by using the Internet.

Tributary A river that joins a larger river.

United Nations (UN) An international peace-keeping organization.

FURTHER INFORMATION

BOOKS TO READ:

Eyewitness Travel Guide: Italy. Rev. ed. New York: Dorling Kindersley, 2003. A travel guide with many maps, cross-section drawings of buildings and excellent photographs of Italy.

Morley, Jacqueline. *A Renaissance Town*. Lincolnwood, Illinois: Peter Bedrick Books, 2001. An illustrated reference featuring fifteenth-century Florence, an archetypal Renaissance town.

Napoli, Donna Jo. *Daughter of Venice*. New York: Wendy Lamb Books, 2002. The fictional story of a young noble girl in sixteenth-century Venice, just after the Renaissance period.

WEBSITES:

GENERAL INFORMATION:

CIA World Factbook
www.cia.gov/cia/publications/factbook/geos/it.html
A variety of up-to-date information on Italy.

Italian Embassy website
www.embitaly.org.uk
Information on the history, the regions and the cities of Italy.

NATIONAL PARKS:

www.parks.it/indice/NatParks.html
This website provides a variety of information, photos and links to Italian national parks.

EUROPEAN UNION:

Europa
www.europa.eu.int/
A website that has links to institutions, information, the latest news and an excellent statistics section.

TOURIST INFORMATION:

Italian Tourist Board
www.enit.it/default.asp?Lang=UK
An information site for nature, history, art and tours within Italy.

PO RIVER:

Po River Basin Authority
www.adbpo.it/inglese/testouk.html
Provides information on the management of Italy's longest river and its tributaries.

METRIC CONVERSION TABLE

To convert	to	do this
mm (millimeters)	inches	divide by 25.4
cm (centimeters)	inches	divide by 2.54
m (meters)	feet	multiply by 3.281
m (meters)	yards	multiply by 1.094
km (kilometers)	yards	multiply by 1094
km (kilometers)	miles	divide by 1.6093
kilometers per hour	miles per hour	divide by 1.6093
cm² (square centimeters)	square inches	divide by 6.452
m² (square meters)	square feet	multiply by 10.76
m² (square meters)	square yards	multiply by 1.196
km² (square kilometers)	square miles	divide by 2.59
km² (square kilometers)	acres	multiply by 247.1
hectares	acres	multiply by 2.471
cm³ (cubic centimeters)	cubic inches	multiply by 16.387
m³ (cubic meters)	cubic yards	multiply by 1.308
l (liters)	pints	multiply by 2.113
l (liters)	gallons	divide by 3.785
g (grams)	ounces	divide by 28.329
kg (kilograms)	pounds	multiply by 2.205
metric tonnes	short tons	multiply by 1.1023
metric tonnes	long tons	multiply by 0.9842
BTUs (British thermal units)	kWh (kilowatt-hours)	divide by 3,415.3
watts	horsepower	multiply by 0.001341
kWh (kilowatt-hours)	horsepower-hours	multiply by 1.341
MW (megawatts)	horsepower	multiply by 1,341
gigawatts per hour	horsepower per hour	multiply by 1,341,000
°C (degrees Celsius)	°F (degrees Fahrenheit)	multiply by 1.8 then add 32

A market trader sets up his stall in Palermo.

Numbers shown in **bold** refer to pages with maps, graphic illustrations or photographs.

The leaning tower of Pisa is one of Italy's most famous tourist attractions.

Tourists enjoy a trip on a gondola in Venice.